A single day lived in virtuous meditation is better than a hundred years lived unbalanced.

—Buddha

The rhythmic forms to which the environment gives rise seem to pass through the autonomic system, into and out of the subconscious without our having once become intellectually aware of them. Rhythm, then, in so far as it affects our poetic mode, has nothing to do with the intellectual life.

—Mary Hunter Austin,
The American Rhythm, 1923

These are the things I know: the slow, summer motion of the air, the shadows that gather upon the walls, birds crisscrossing the screen, the rhythms within me.

—N. Scott Momaday, recounting his boyhood,
The Names, 1976

For the poet the anguishing question—and it is indeed the subject of the poem—is: how can one not only speak of Being, but say Being itself. Poetry is the experience of this question.

—Paul De Man,
*Blindness and Insight: Essays in the Rhetoric
of Contemporary Criticism*, 1983

Also by **Jeff Davis**

Speaking of Mother Earth

RESERVOIR

Poems by Jeff Davis

Barnburner Press
1910 Mecca • Dallas, Texas 75206

Acknowledgements

A special thanks to Robert Trammell and Frederick Turner
for reading with care and having faith in this manuscript;
to Jennifer Polavieja and Adrienne Cox-Trammell for
realizing this project; and to John McMurphy, Jimmy Davis,
and Bill Burford for their generous support of and faith in
this project.

"For the Recovery of Hearing: A Prayer in Couplets" was published in
Lightning & Ash No. 1, 1996.

Library of Congress Cataloging-in-Publication
Data Davis, Jeff.

TABLE OF CONTENTS

TABLE OF CONTENTS

The Aqueduct of Poetry
An Introduction to Jeff Davis's City Reservoir   Frederick Turner

City Reservoir is a pipeline that runs from the wells of subjective dream through the passages of myth and disciplined poetic form to a grave and charming statement of public moral philosophy. It is divided into two sections: the first, a stream of personal consciousness—raw, chaotic, inconsequential but numinous; the second, a rich, controlled meditation upon the landmarks, people, history, and spirit of the city of Dallas. It is a gift to Dallas—this new city, sprung up on the sun-baked prairie out of the dreams and nightmares of two million energetic people drawn from the ends of Earth and forced to invent themselves a landscape. This invented landscape Davis has made into his own Lake District, his own concrete-edged Arcadia.

Davis believes—rightly, I think—that poets feed the city and quench its drouth by giving it eyes and ears, criticism that understands its spirit, love, and an undercurrent of dream life. Dallas has few cellars, because of its peculiar geology and economics; Davis digs metaphysical cellars, and begins to lay down its wine. Coming from such a relatively new poet, the book is remarkably mature in its style and organization; it is almost a single poem. Though Davis has learned from the Dallas poets—from the wise and mystical Robert Trammell, from the quirky and perceptive Michael Helsem, and from my own odd efforts at uniting the classical and the futuristic—he has a voice that is uniquely his own. What is especially exciting about him is his growing awareness of the sonic potential of poetic form, and his brilliant analysis of the sounds and inner meanings of words. His puns, sometimes taking up whole sentences, reveal what the wisdom of language is trying to tell us. The reader needs to pause with these flashes of linguistic brilliance, these strange and musical variations of word-fragments coalescing toward meaning; they are the crucial stage of transformation from mere subjective association to valuable meaning. Language itself guides us from the irresponsible fertility of dream to the weight and moral integrity of public statement, but it can only do so through the recombinations and intercourse of poetry. This is why a new city, with but little poetry as yet to call its own, needs its poets so dearly.

Davis's message is not, however, just for Dallas. It is for all of Texas, and for America as a whole. The myth of Pegasus, to which Davis refers several times, has been adopted by the city of Dallas as its own (The Mobil corporate symbol of the flying horse has long been a landmark of the downtown district, and it has more recently been interpreted in a sculpture park and fountain, conceived by the Dallas Institute of Humanities and Culture). But its story—how the divine winged horse sprang from the blood of the hideous slain Medusa, and how when its hoof struck the earth a spring bubbled forth to form the fountain Hippocrene, from which all poets drink—is one which has value for the state and the nation as well. Davis sees Dallas—warts, commerce, traffic, dispossessed Indians, and all—and loves it; and ours is a civilization that needs to be seen and loved into being.

Waking Up

Hold on to this in moving through:
through the blinds see overgrown
grass wet from last night's storm, a pear tree

pink in bloom. Take them
for what they are worth.

Take a deep breath the same way,
a recoiling loop centered in
each moment's rhythm, a wind
that sends an eye, less than a flapping sail, in

upon itself and out again. Then, breathe out:
the need to bear witness upon the world,
the world's need of seeing and of
being seen.

Falling Asleep

I often try to fall asleep like this: looking
through the window for the next day and
trying to see what I could make happen
that would make the morning
less heavy.

What Motivates Us to Get Up

Somebody's knocking in the dark. It's me
dressed as a caballero, and someone
on the inside thinks I've come to get her.
She won't get out of bed to answer.

A motivational speaker says he has answers
in music and in stories for our stress.
Music makes us fe-e-el go-o-od.
Use it, he says, for your stress, and something

in the way he says "Use it" strips rhythm
of what motivates me since symphonies
don't have soundbites, and Sun Dances
don't have jingles. Practice staying light,

he says, on the surface. Don't break a sweat.
"Tonto always got a whipping," he says
to make some point. His words illustrate
and move us to an end. Get it? A tale

for every occasion. I leave the session sensing
something, someone is drawing blood from us.
Consultants can be vampires. Security systems
in our houses hold emotions

in tact. Rhythms of a stadium scoreboard
provide the city with excitement, and no sweat.
Break a sweat. Score a sweat. And why work,
if it doesn't work for you? Sweat

for something else, some new song
or rhythm knocking on a door.
The story, the simple one, the one
that motivates, lives next door. My neighbor
wakes his boys near three AM
on some mornings to take them for a drive

in his wild Mustang down country streeets
with no lights, surfing a road at sixty maybe seventy
miles per hour and the boys, in their half dreaming,
slip-streaming shaking, are breathless and numb
and dumb. No talking's allowed, the tires hum loud,
down black ocean roads. To the tires' rhythm,
the boys' heads nod and the old man hums some
Parker tune, Driftin' on a Reed or Crazeology,
some ritual madness among the black tide roads.

This, he will tell his sons, is how you drive
through dreams, how you find the seams
in a day's work and give yourself a chance,
while laying bricks in the heat along someone else's
immaculate swimming pool, to fly in a day:
Break a sweat every moment. Fan each breath,

catch your breath as if you were trying to
hold it near your chest so it could feel
your heartbeat. There must be a way
to let today slip through cracked doors.

When they drive up near dawn,
the two boys open the doors and shoot down
the street and wail like laughing birds
stuck in a cat's throat, their madness
shocked and suppressed in the break of day.
Time to get up.

To Swim Through the Day

Don't worry, just swim, hand slides in.
Do you want dessert, hand slides in, swim.
We mixed up the serial numbers
for your breakfast.

You make my eighteenth unit, united we
buy, consume a dog in a cage puddling
slobber from her jawbone. She's never seen

another dog. We high-rise live, the lady
says. We high-rise live, she says again
in an elevated voice. Who signed on
with the Jets? Everyone wants to be

a goalie but no one wants to keep score anymore.
The World Cup did those kids a world of good.
I get to walk in the rain, cup it in my hands,

cup the world in my ears, vestibules for the earth.
Rain on your living room for posterity. Make room
in your fingers to give a dog a bath. Scrub a wet
coat. Soak a hide. Hide nails in a scalp.

Scrub lather wishes away and embrace suds.
When you embrace a scrubbing, things besides fleas
fall away and nothing comes to you through

a faucet. Soft it. A soft faucet. Hard-tapped
water. Pass it on to neighbors that paint
their lawns green. Rauschenberg sleeps in
paint, and goats follow him to bed.

He once sought the Goathead and found it
in a cube of cheese. Don't say you remember
anything. Remember is a lie, head member

of the Liar's Club. Fatten is. Slim was.
Toss a rock through yesterday. A broken
window already and it only cuts fingers.
Scare the man who says he's old from

his recliner and force him onto the porch to face
a shotgun wedding to the earth. No, fanatics
need not unite, no more shotgun weddings,

no more shotgun beliefs, no more shotgun
changes. American leaders want their voters
to be dumber than they are. Why do intelligent
people like you bother with poetry?

Electrons exist everywhere at the same time
because they are really the same. There's really
just one electron moving so fast it just seems infinite.

Matter is solid because probability patterns are difficult
to compress. Doors of perception as they are are
infinitely bewildering. We are one inseparable web
of relationships. Fan blades spin so fast

I can see what's behind them. Goethe wasn't
such a crank. A woman in a blue robe scratches
a bush's back with a rake, her son sleeps in

the evening, his three children run yell play
bassboom from a car stereo boom the street
rakescratch streetboom rakescratch boyspeed
streetboom rake scratch we children

fill space and rake mountains and hope for a moment
we connect and become a new equation
raked from street debris, become cold grass for a moment,

cool, getting darker, Stop that yellin'! Cool hums. Dark
bleeds, seeps, crawls tall across the grass belly one
slow big gulp at a time, slowly swallows rakescratch
slowly scratches streetboom, swallows boyspeed,

darkness washes in a nightsea   nightsea
blindlight   and nightsea
swim and hold hands in a nightsea

The Day Is Fixed

You miss it. You don't have the nerve
anymore to shoot. Old man blackmails
Phil Gramm. I miss the details.
Gramm will have him killed and rig the election.

Get a stool this morning. Damp
shirts and jeans and underwear
clothe wire lines and mock scare-
crows. Mockingbirds scare crows.

Crows mock clothes, socks mock feet,
rotted peaches on the street.
Stock a smock
for the day's post-heat.

Dead skin flakes. A baby stroller
slowly moves. Bicycles circle.
Birds bathe in dirt. Woman
with pantyhose hat waters her yard.

He turned us down. Hang in there.
They check around. I don't know
for sure, but I'll keep you posted.
You gonna be around? Don't hit the ceiling.

Dog-day post-heat, crows work through noon.
Sun stiffens towel. Some shoot hoops,
some shoot hope, and some shoot dope.
They are fixes, like shopping

the other side of the river. Fix yourself.
Fix it. Get your fix on Route 666.
Get your fix on the word fix. Let it fix
itself. Let it fix itself in you: a bur

by a clothespin stuck on your sock.
Carry fix with you. Fix
is a kami. Make it stick.
Socket kami. Give it a plug

for an election on the next talk
show. Give a fix benefit.
To ignore or to abuse words
is a crime, and Gramm is a criminal cracker.

The history of plagiarism tells the story of word
thieves and word crimes. Crime rhyme.
Rhyme crime. Re: hym. Re: cim.
Ray hym. Race him

so he won't win the election. Say
a sun prayer and steal a last ray for the day,
steal a wave, steal a glance at lanced steel.
Stieglitz and Man Ray took from the day's heaps.

Oh, say, can you steal!
Brother can you spare a crime?

Light through blinds stripes lawns. Steals.
Light through blinds stripes lawns. Stripes
trip and yawn across the street.　　Blind
through light lawn steals

light blind　　blindlight　　blindlight

Putting Things Together:
Twin Forms of a Dallas Day

I run through a campus and hide from twins,
my sisters, or friends. I have shot someone
from a tower and hide behind bike
stands. The twins stand some twenty feet
away. "I want to look for my brother. Does that mean

anything to you," Adrienne says. She runs away.
Jennifer shrugs, spots me, and says
"I'm glad you stopped running and hiding."
She calls me Lee Harvey and puts her arm
around me as she escorts me to the cops.

Adrienne's boyfriend is almost finished
with his book of poetry concerning Dallas.
We speak of the need for a form for a forum.
Forum for form to bring poets in this city together.
It will be a trick. Something in the city air

won't let me digest the day, any day in whole
as if it has been full. Always running,
either hiding or trying to get somewhere
fast so the day can rest tomorrow.
Day kills itself. The city's horse

was born in blood from the necks
of slaughtered natives. Perhaps Fortress
Worth was its twin goldsword. Pollux and Castor
won't be around the sky for a while. Oil on a Dallas salad.
Pollock finally stopped using oils after part of his brain

had rotted from trying to make art in Manhattan.
He never visited Dallas where there are
manhole covers in this city's sky,
where holes cover this city's sky.
Holy sky. Holy sky. O to be whole!

Dallas Reservoir

The beards need trimming, the sexton says.
Churches now have dress codes, and so the men
with ragged beards are turned away.
A dream perhaps but still I wonder
what gives me access to a temple in the city.

Dallas could use a reservoir or two
in the center of downtown. In the middle of August
I grow delirious wishing for this city.
Someone once said something crass like
if you make a lake, swans will come.
It's hard work, this lake making,
but something in the asphalt and in the motion
of ongoing work and of being near people,
here and here, must give way upon occasion
to the language of swans.

Some woman named Leda knew how swans feel,
the way Zeus wrapped his wings around her
and plunged deep inside, but that's a story
for another city. I have been looking
instead for a rabbi named Rauschenberg
who could transform a stapler
with a mailing label to a stranger
named Chris Kraft stuck on its back
into a swan pond. The simplest tool
becomes a way to make a place
of prepositions and
of propositions where women make lakes
where women make lakes make love
where women in the middle of cities
make lakes make love.

Lake call early in the morning. A mist.
A wish. A lost Canadian goose hovers

over White Rock Lake. After an hour
it rests on a wet black bough
and speaks to ducks for now.
Between the flap of the wing and the glide
the shadow falls.
Between the mist and the wish
between the ground and the sound
content geese make peace with an old lake.

A wish. A bastard wish. Millie,
a doleful woman who works the register
at the Kwik Kar Lube room up the street, says
"It's hot. But it's not just hot
anymore. It's the ozone and everything.
It's not just hot anymore. You know?"
I nod and say "It's not just hot anymore."

She hates the anxiety that hangs in this city
in August. Like being locked in a sauna
that travels wherever you go.
She stares out the window and says gravely
"I like salads in hot weather."

salads in hot weather
salads in Dallas
Dallas salads
peppered with breadsticks
that stretch beyond the highest dollar sign.
There is comfort in commerce.
There is safety in complaint.

Millie goes home with me
once a month to trim my beard.
In the backyard we wait for the heat to settle
somewhere in the throats of crickets.
Spots in trees and spots in space cricket
the air

cricket   ricket   rick   ritt
hairy antennae send signals
to the rooftop next door.

A wolf's head appears in a cloud and covers the moon
that becomes the wolf-cloud's left eye
as it dreams of a woman named Millie
who likes to eat fruit salad in hot weather.
The woman in the wolf's dream drinks tea
from tea leaves from tree leaves
and says to whomever is listening,
Birds leave trees and return.

This, Millie says, is what we do.
We prepare
to return. We ready ourselves and the earth,
we lay the groundwork and make lakes
to return home where moons will fall
from our tongues as we embrace
our mother and our father. It's a loop.

The wolf hears her and moves on,
and the woman under the roof next door
hears her and shuts her metal shades.
That's all you do to enter a sacred temple,
she says as she snips the loose ends of my beard.
Somehow it just doesn't sound like enough, or else
it sounds too familiar. But still
I thank her and tip her and ask her
to come back next month.

Assertions

"You are curious," someone says. My cousin
and I duck my father's flashlights. A dream stamped

"FOR YOUR REVIEW," 124 padded envelopes
stuffed with books. In early morning numbness
a new dog's collar jingles as she licks her stitches.

Contain yourself from laughter. CONTAIN YOURSELF
in a sack, in a bottle, in a jar. Womb. Job. Someone
said "lover." In another "thought." THAT is all bliss

of everykind; Attaining this bliss
one realizes his nature which is
all bliss, so say Upanishads.

In itself, space has no limits or boundaries … Man
constructs a geometry, Euclidean or non-Euclidean,
and decides to view space in those terms, says Suzi Gablik.

Files Scanned: 75. Someone says
"I can't believe I got a hold
of you." People are falling out

of the sky for that position. You need
to eat meat. Go eat a carrot,
my neurotic grandmother says.

Man constructs a geometry.
Stress constricts a vein.
Tear rows of stamps, tinted red, tinted blue.

Dog licks stitches. Tongue licks
stamps. Stamps stick
to tongue. Sticky tongue
stamps lick. Left hand
sticks red 5 cents. Right
hand sticks blue dollar.

Body is a system. Man
constructs a geometry. Tongue
licks stitches. Stamp stitches.

Time licked. Tongue stamped.
Time stuck. Arms tinted red
by fluorescent light and sun

the other day when hiking
through Arapaho Pass. Valley
u-shaped from glacier's pass

some 10,000 years ago. Valley stamped.
Lake Dorothy stamped and contained
among snow-coated mountains,

in my reddened arms, my naked
toes, my licked tongue: Contain
yourself. Contain a mountain

in your calves and chest. Body is
a system with its own geometry
and geography. Mine a stamp

for every cent and scent.
Scents stamp our
desire. Scents rise.

Sire sends a word at dusk
upon the heron's beak:
Sayanora. Since it must be

so. So scents must be it. So
be. Be it. THAT is bliss. Be
bliss. Kiss bliss. Sick bliss

on dis-ease. Ease dis
sickness, Bliss.
The dog squats and sniffs,

squats and sniffs,
licks and squats.
Cumquats for a nose.

Requiem for curiosity. Cure
for curiosity. You are curious.
You are cured and ready to be

preserved. You are cured bliss.
You cure bliss. You are bliss.
Moon of the Moulting appears.

My jaw tightens. Moonjaw   MoonjawMoonja
Stick stamps on envelopes overlooked
this morning   moonja

Moonja is curious Moonja is curious Moonja   cure

To Get Here from Here

I think I oversleep so I don't make it
to someone else's church. But it's 8 AM
not 3 PM. I don't make it
to Joe's lakehouse either. It's late,
raining, and I don't know how to get
there from here.

It takes a while to get here near a sutty
still stream where a crow caws, a saw
hums, and ignored voices surface again.
Again, like morning, breaking away,
so here is morning, dawn, a dawning breaking
past noon.

An airplane rattles by, but no one there sees me.
Dragonflies do it in the fuzzy stream,
an insect version of From Here to Eternity.
I feel closer to the heavens than if I were in
a rattling airplane. Some dude's laughter breaks in
the air. Another dawning.

Dawn happens
now and now.
I am here.
Where am I
when I am
not here?

I want to be here
on the job
in crowded hallways, in
busy rooms, in
heated talks, in

committee meetings.

I want to meet here
and now, to be here
anywhere where dawn
happens. Place this place
in hallways and rooms. Place
earth in hallways and corporate buildings.

Erase traces of rooms from rivers, streams,
and lakes that are hard to find. Tree roots
grow through a streamline boulder. Tree roots
break through. Break roots. Root this in
hallways and rooms. Place rocks in building
bedrocks. Instincts break through appointments:

The stream keeps
running. I am here
now and now.
A leaf from another fall streams.

Someone dreams a leaf falls and
a leaf falls.

Someone dreams a stream leaves
a park and falls into place
in crowded hallways and clouded board rooms.

I fall into place
streaming here
now and now.

Thump, thump, thump.
A basketball thumps where young men
let noon and afterwards pass, slip
by like a leaf streaming over stones.

Thump, thump, thump,

the slow rhythm, of hangin' on
to summer noons.

They jazz june
and stream through a day one way.

To be where dawn breaks
now and now
changes a day's tone.

To think of being here
does not have to be
different from being here.

To think of being here
can bring me here.

An ant bites the webbed skin between
two fingers here. I flick it and it falls
with brittle leaves into the stream

lined with Coca-Cola cups, a trash bag, a
classified ad for cars, bottle caps, dreams, cans.

Here is here
physical within
of organs
organic.
Wind blows in leaves.
Leaves feel wind in their veins.
Wind veins vein wind.

Of metal and faint sewage
swirl around this small walking bridge
where another flicked ant flies.
Air barks and whistles and hums and creaks

crowded space. Butterfly,
yellow and black dots, some name.

And suddenly to this, ironed up over irons
and lamps, heavy with objects
burning down the house. There is caution and
false peace that covers emptiness in this house.
Tree roots push through boulders and in writing
"false peace" peace persists. Surprise.

Morning dawns in the inside of your thighs
and brings me here streamlined and finding
my way to a lake.

Housed

I am walking toward a soft house, organic.
It grows in the woods. Someone told me
you can grow houses now and buildings.
He says it will take some planning.

The yard is being treated for ticks. Treat it well.
The dog is being washed, and people
across the street chuckle at the wet dog's coat.
Fifteen or more of them have gathered

from nowhere. Trucks and cars along the street.
They're wearing black and they're laughing
at the dog's water-pressed coat. Someone
has died, and I don't know who.

I hear that North Korea wants to pressure
the U.S. into twelve-tone maybe fifteen-tone
compositions. Divide an octave or a treaty
by fifteen. Stay tuned and in tune to be

an out-of-tune tone. I have been that.
I go where Roe reads, and someone yells
"Jesus loves you" and "You lied when you said
you were raped." Amazing what people

say they know. "The Lips of the Wise"
often stay still. Couth yellow candles
are smoking what we consume. A
protester's words seep in, second-hand.
Words are coated. Some words coat
our throats. Others strip them
and make us hoarse. Someone says
some words fly in the air, but

his are not not those words they say do.
Words they say fly often have heavy bodies,

bomber bodies built to break the sound barrier.
Small words lodge themselves.

"Famine," Amend separation. Mend
hunger. "I will lose my grasp," But grasp
it. Can I? An actor's words
we speak mostly. Soft spoken.

Salty. And what does the world matter
with affected emotion. Last chance to peek
at what swims in the tongue: mythic medic,
mythic method, Pythagorean.

Mythpit sweat. Shirts sweat
sweat shirts. Give the sweat off your back
for the man across the street
where people had gathered this morning.

Across the street street light lights the lawn.
Lawn bags bag disposal. Disposed tree branches
branch the curb. A man is curbed inside.
A man alone in bed is curbed inside the house

across the street. In the window a candle.
It is not enough to notice we need growth.

Bless his house, his daily bread. Bless him
whom I do not know.

Tidy Up

Have you no convictions? Have you never been convicted?
Watch what you watch closely. It enters your dreams
and becomes you, tries to flatter you, or check you.

Always the clock on the nightstand is the first thing
I check so throughout the day I count on those numbers
and the coffee machine to work with regularity.

Phone rings with regular space between bells.
A friend says he must get his mouth reworked
today. He has an appointment to rework his mouth.

He tells me he leaves for places early to be
ahead of time. To be ahead, I guess, we each
create different strategies. A cat sits by a screen door

and sees jungle movements in front yard shrubs.
When I was a boy, I sat on a ledge that overlooked
a boulevard and across the boulevard a railroad track
and across the track miles of fields and wooded lots

with horses grazing and herons stalking. I saw places
where wild things lived in the city, wild without
violence. The cat watches bugs and lizards and hears

children chatter. The cat stoops low, ready to spring,
a house cougar screened in, ready to pounce upon a cicada
lost from last night. But the cicada passes

and the cat turns to play instead with a rubberband.
Some of us would like our world tamer even
than this, to have sutures where incisors and guts once were.

Content to keep clean and screened, held in
check by clocks. Clean screens clock
our keeps. Speak lean tocks near filed cans.

Necrolife. File life. Feline life. Defiled life
kneels in dust near plywood trees and tinseled grass.
Screen your calls and stay to the clock.

Listen to the clockcalls. The clock calls.
We have rhythms for getting ready
for appointments, the solemn, steady

preparation for some happening, a new phase
like the changing of summer to fall when fishers
clean their boats and farmers ready their machines.

Surgeons scrub their hands before surgery
and after murder. Lady Macbeth licks her
bandages and scans her sutures like braille

before going home. That is what dusting's for —
this grooming and sweeping and primping
and straightening and making rooms seem other

than what they were — deposits or debris the tides
left behind. It's all preparation for going home.
Write this line to prepare for sleep. There. Nothing.

Direction of Art

At night the hallway is a path
in Colorado. Someone slams
a cafeteria tray, and I didn't go
down the right escalator.

At the lake pebbles blister my toes.
Skin loosens and bubbles. Girls wrestle
in the mud to find their animals.
Mud must have been a first paint:

babypaint to find an animal. Send a kid
to China through a mudhole. Send a kid
to private or public school. A friend debates:
Private or public, paper or plastic,

private or public, paper or plastic,
we have choices. Save the world in choices.
Save yourself in art. A person scribbles
sketches in her basement. They are dis-

covered and exposed on a gallery wall.
Emily Dickinson stayed indoors. Private
or public, paper or plastic. A father threw
his son's dirty underwear on his girlfriend's

front porch for revenge. Rustic Circles in
the newspapers in the bathrooms. A wedding
announcement under a pillow. A poetry
reading. A mountain or a canvas. A tree or a poem.
Become indignant to save a soul from slipping
in an armchair. No one said it would be easy.
Listen closely, and I'll tell you a story.
Imagine being eighty-six and never being able

to vote. South Africa is changing. Radio drama
is natural for us. Our roots are in poetry.

Be practical, someone said, and stop painting
other painters. Paint for commodity instead.

Duchamp's commode signed R. Mutt is expensive.
Take a myth, for instance. Take a myth.
How does someone take a myth
from someone else? Mythos or money?
Mythos or money, paper or plastic, private or public.
Moonja has come early today. Moonja has come
before the earth turns my back on the sun.
Moonja wants space Moonja says

do art to change the world. Artist at the center. Drum
for the homeless. Drum for the homeless
and save a soul from slipping down
an armchair. Drum to save a myth. Drum

to save a myth. Build and paint a scrappy cover
for a baglady. Drama. For the people.
Drum for the people. Drum drama.
Drum up some business for mythos.

Money or mythos.
Hallways are pathways to mountains.
Ways mount in halls hallmount hallmount
You can walk down my hall anytime.
You can walk up my path anytime.
Mountains are not owned. Don't fence yourself
in. Myths are not owned. Don't fence yourself in.
Private or public, paper or plastic, mythos or money,

hallways to mountains. Moonja comes
without the moon tonight. Biplane engine
hums and swoons tonight. "The bird that succeeds
is the one that gets an office ... with a phone number

that'll be easy for patients
to remember!" Moonja medicine.
Medicine or money. Medicine money.
Medicine myth. Mythic medicine. Medium

Medicine. Medic mythic. Mythic medic.
Science or medicine,
mythic
medic.

Ars Poetica Today

I am caught cut-and-pasting names
of some 100 people on a party circuit:
circus: Circe: parties are sirens. Something
more is calling, an incoherent, formless melody.

My sister says she partied all night,
but her body can't take it anymore.
"Had we but world enough, and time,
This partying, lady, were no crime."

We've listened with marvel to poets
being drunk all day, so we fear we'll miss
the big moment if we nap. We cannot
part from old terms and syntax easily.

Old cans easily part the terms
of ice crystallized on broccoli stalks.
Cat thumps cardboard.
Window fans.

Supper storm grumbles. Pasta broils.
Water bubbles. Don't mistake connotation
for genuine emotion when little if any
real emotion rises to the top.
Only concentration centers on a trait
and centers on cons of thought,
the way thought pretends to be
observation. Keep thought at the top
where crumbs crust and collect
for roaches' supper. Keep thought
at the surface to ground it
in senses. Refrigerator hums.
The sink shakes from thunder.

Drizzle drizzles on a screen. Fingers
on a wooden table somewhere

cannot stay here forever. Not world enough.
It's still raining in Angola. The Dalai Lama's
exiled. Omission has become an institution.
Don't mistake connotation for devotion.

Sustain thought. Sniff persistently.
If art is to be sustained
thought must be sustained.
If art is to be sustained abstract thought must
be sustained. There is a difference
where–no–how thoughts are lined. A jolt.
I must become a convict if not
to "I" then to a sense of words,
and to place. Fragments
may be more oracular
than orchestrated syntax and
enjambed lines. Enjambment
hints at pensiveness. Fragments

ease down ears. This is a turn: Necessary:
To utter moonja in public then I will
have to sustain private lines. Private
lines rivet river bolts and connect to
Moonja, moon operator who works
the boat on the lagoon and speaks
lagoon lingo. Storms brew and without

direction they can scatter and leave
behind only junkheaps of bird parts,
branches, sporadic breaths that try to form
into something tangible: air tries to become
soil. Someone could create a paper moon
more real than the chunk of rock the Eagle
flew to. If not a paper moon, then a paper

lagoon. Resolved to formulate some
thing of Mallarmé-Rilke-Eliot-Stevens-Williams-
Pound-Olson-Creeley-Simic-Berryman-
Neruda-Rwanda-Maronage.
Project self, sustain self,
and refrain, refrain, refrain,
from too much abstraction

from too much communing and immune
self to too much understanding to too much
helping or being socially relevant.
Poet at the center: will it work?
What's the point, poet?
What's the cure, poet?
Where is a cure?

Counting

The loan officer
cannot give me exact figures
until he has the exact payoff amount.
It may be a day. It may be a week.

Loan it, loan something, like time,
or simply give it away and make a pot-
latch in the city. Keep on giving off.

Forget computing in your best interest.
Rate giving away without percentages.
Roll back the numbers, cover them with sand and
let tides swallow them and leave them
marooned with oil drillers on a steel ship.
Do this in the name of economy
and in the name of those stranded in the city.
Listen to the youth speak of their cryptic lives.

Let them open vaults: a different way
of banking. Let them remove simple stitches
from the sutures in their bellies:

from the marooned in the city. The marooned
people of Suriname, deep in the Caribbean,
still live in forests and still sing and
still dance their earth beat, earthdrum,
earthstrum, heartstrum, earthstrum,
moving with the tides, still moving

behind the leaves. Hear them, birds
chattering outside our windows. Hear them.
Hear them. Earthstrum. Heartstrum.

Moonja leads them. Moonja hears them.
There are stories of fingernail moons.
I cannot wash my hands from them.

●   ●   ●

I am a convict who has told corrupt tales how
somewhere, near Rome I think, a confused
and aging man had made a desperate attempt
to make his mark, to fool the mortal laws.
So he stole the woman's rhythms—or bought them
in a brothel (I can't recall)—and forged them

with some metal strips and straps. Under
the moon in Rome, he placed the parts and straps,
the straps and parts, upon a beach and waited.
Upon the first "midnight," some say, I think,
the metal contraption began to click,
to click, to click, to click, to click. At first

at random, and then, as minutes passed,
as we now say, the steel machine began
to click and tick, to beat and beat on cue.

The man could count the space between the clicks
more precisely than the pause between
the tides that touched and left his feet. To leave

his footprints in the sand, the cliché goes,
he left the world a governor for all time.
Someone once told me she had heard the man

had been a mathematician and a poet
who lived in an Italian monastery.
Day after day, he had sought, some say, some way

to tell him when to pray upon the hour,
but I have heard, as well, that he had sought
a new poetics, a form to alter the way

we live and move and dance and work, a form
of being that would let us reach eternity
and infinity here
and here and now and now. We would embrace
each hum, each creak, each moment of a storm,
and each embrace would make us immortal

for a moment. But year after year, they say,
poem after poem, forms and lovers and words
slipped away. Nothing new would come.

He could not unleash the form that would allow
people to sense the gods in their hands, their tools,
their narrow streets, their shady homes, in dusk.

After a while, he felt foolish fooling
with numbers and words for so long. Be real,
someone in so many words said to him.

Math and poetry make not a stinking difference
in our lives. Make something, build something
real that we can put our hands on, covet, buy or steal

to make our lives a tad easier to endure.
Pillows, casting irons, foot stools,
and saddles, these are things we can reproduce

and sell and trade to improve our lives.
The villagers had told him this, and thus
the poet-mathematician abandoned form

in words and numbers and thought instead
of forms in products. So, so the story goes,
he took rhythms from women who spun wool

through the night and made a clock. Moonja
has been sleepless ever since that night that moon's light
blessed the instrument that has thrown the tides
off balance. What balance? Want balance?
Slip away, slip away, the answer on our lips,
slip away, slip away, Dixie Land.

Moonja moves and sways your hips, slip away.
You sense the tides are coming, you sense
the tides are turning. Slip away. See it

in a limestone rock sitting on a nightstand.
See it in the pennies dripping in the sand.
It won't go away, so slip away with it.

Let Moonja's lips slip into your mouth,
stretch it wide. Let the nighttide in.
Simple way to save the day: let the nighttide in.

The time is here: Time is here.
The place is now: Place is now.
Nighttide rolls in: count the space.

You won't be late: count the space
then let the numbers roll away
into Moonja's mouth. Swallow

whole numbers, integers, let them swim
in the belly, bellytide, bellytide.
Up, and, through, and, with, and, in in.

Restless

Restless, some intruder again
but again almost mostly lost.

Rhythms appear in handwriting, or, rather,
handwriting reveals body-mind rhythms.

Vestiges

Suddenly nothing and everything disappears
and appears. A clock had been knocked off
a stand. A hotel room got lost in a motel
parking lot.

Fruit Flies with Altered DNA Molecules

have different Circadian rhythms.
A gene of 7,000 bases, a mutant, some slight change,
a T to an A, changes the way a fly flies through day
and night. "Timing is in our genes."
"What kind of world are we living in when the seasons
don't affect us? We are animals, after all."

Is this a test? How will you perform?

If for Once He Could Seize the Trumpet Vine

by the throat and squeeze out a simple line
perhaps in time he could discover how
he could walk in measure with the day's Tao.

I Still Think the Word was a Pun

No one gets it though because it was spoken
in a dead language. Puns, you know, are timely.

For the Recovery of Hearing:
A Prayer in Couplets

Someone whispers in her husband's ear
something about it being time to fly.

More airline for your money.
Slow traffic over the Trinity.

Someone shot a doctor for performing
abortions. This magic show has been cancelled.

Someone stole a portrait of Thomas Jefferson.
Investing is a form of thievery and vice-versa:

reversible vices. This city invests in vices
and desires disposable income.

Hören, zu-hören, Holderlin.
"And what are poets for in a destitute time?"

To recover the ear. "Poets are the mortals who, singing
earnestly of the wine-god, sense the trace

of the fugitive gods, stay on the god's tracks and so trace
for their kindred mortals the way toward turning,"

Hear that which arises, feel the draft,
a butterfly wing: "A breath for nothing. An afflatus

in the god. A wind." Hallowed ear.
"Why are they silent, too, the theatres

[and the nightclubs of Dallas] ancient and hallowed?"
Hallowed be thine ear. Allow a hear.
Allow an ear to be wedded to a heartstring,
an earthstring. Earthstring strum.

Phonestrum: hear the voices in the mail and on the phone
guarantee your signature: verify your approval.

Wir, Gewaltsamen, wir währen länger,
Aber wann, in welchem aller Leben,

sind wir endlich offen und Empfänger?
We violent ones remain a little longer.

Ah but when, in which of all our lives,
shall we at last be open and receivers?

Receive us not unto a plush red velvet congregational bench
and purchase large candles in our names.

Sign a postcard with a picture of Notre Dame
then guarantee your signature with your voice.

A pulse beats in names. A pulse beats in games
and in magic shows. Doctor, doctor,

lead us not unto contemplation and deliver
our babies express mail guaranteed overnight service.

Allow an ear to be wedded
to a heartstring, an earthstring.

Strum. Earthstrum.
Earthdrum. Eardrum.

Still the dark cloud-coughing sky, doctor.
Still the dome. Still the steeple.

Still the strum of sticks and soil.
Still the cries. Still earth cries.   Still earth cries

Sleep Peels for
Daytime Doctors

On an old high school patio yearbook pictures of dead
classmates stand as monolithic walls. I try to get out.

Doctors at Parkland make three holes in a girl's gut to let
an infection leak. Leeches cure and drain.

"Then for half an hour did Dr. Arrowsmith and
Dr. Marchard, forgetting the plague, forgetting

the more cruel plague of... fear, draw diagrams."
Plagues break out. Plagues break us. Plague us.

"Plague": pretend the word is antiquated.
"Fear": ditto. Suture in my head, your head, sew

up the plagues that bug us or them, or us
versus them. Professional white men gather to confer

on what's bothering them. Spears appear
like plagues, they say. "Don't think I've ever

seen a spear or made a living with one."
Hammers, nails, wrenches, sockets, bolts,

how to work with hands and with purpose
drop away from tongues and are forgotten.

Hand it to the computers. Would we be lost
without more naming, washed out with the tides

if we didn't fax ourselves into the next century?
A scientist retreats to her lab

to examine bacilli, her world where Latin thrives
in the active meditation of placing hands

on test tubes and old Bunsen burners.
Spear: her: Bunsen burners: Rwandans.

Parents are dying of AIDS.
Brothers are dying for drugs.

Children are dying from rage
and trying to grow immune to death.

We wish to hold death in our hands. It will not fall
away though or slip out of our memory's party

as do black-tie nights or Club Med gigs.
Someone laughs and says he wants to be

a Club Med intern. Wannabe Intern, turn in
for the night. He will turn in his sleep. Sleep peels

memory. Sleep peels fill the bedroom floors
so we won't forget plagues still exist the morning after.

2

2.

Tempest on an April Night

Ms. Nettles down the street lost her boy
the other night in a random shooting. We all
know it. We can barely say a word. Up and down
the street, on our porches, we wait
for a tempest to roll in. In some new world
a wizard is restless and seizing the moment
for his revenge, and we suffer the reverberations.
A shipwreck once occurred every ten days
in a harbor along the Aegean Sea, when people
counted them and made statistical charts
like they do today with murders, divorces, and disasters
in this neighborhood. Nothing much new

under the sky's brave and dull salmon belly
but a pulsating light flashing every now and then
as if the sky swallowed some radiated airplane
with people seeking light. In Bermuda and
along the Atlantic Coast, four, five hundred years ago,
men braved the storms to find new lands.

For a moment the sky lights up and illuminates
two boys running down the street, laughing,
singing some nonsense song they made up,
two Ariel sprites in the wind.

There's an engine roaring two streets over,
and something in the air is buzzing
that something's not right, something's
still not fair. We sit here, though, waiting,
as if by not fleeing the storm
we gain penance for whatever part we play.

From Thanksgiving Tower

Where are you? Where are you
looking? A man stands on
the seventeenth floor of Thanksgiving
Tower and stares like glass back at
downtown's open face. Little is

transparent about the city's look. Not just tinted
windows or the Trinity's water, or even the people's
gestures in traffic. But the way people live, too,
and walk hides: rhythms that rumble under-
foot. Never had a quiver here, much less
a quake. Don't really get how earth moves
and shakes here. Wouldn't know it if I felt it.

The man in the window puts his hands and
face against the pane as if he were sucking
fresh air through the glass's pores. Officed
in conditioned air, he sees a grid below
and wonders if he could walk along the lines
cartographers use to trace the city, its
remote streams, the neighborhood divisions, its
designated historical spots, the opaque map
of being in the city his only guide.

2

Day and Night in Dallas

Air is thick in Dallas
so we breathe in short gasps.

Wrinkled men in white shirts
shuttle to starched buildings.

Our city glows as we
sing of prosperity.

At midnight our sky stays
white with smutty clouds and

downtown's glimmer, so we
assume we live in light.

Air is thick in Dallas,
so we breathe in short gasps,

and we rarely notice
how day has turned to night.

Wild Angels in Dallas:
A Parable for City-Dwellers

His father let him search for wild angels
in the wooded field down the street when
cicadas heaved and Junebugs buzzed,
darkness dotted by lightning bugs.
No fear of fire from random shootings
or of being stolen by some stranger,
the boy made his way through meeting
a dozen or so angels in the woods
before he was ten.

Twenty years ago in those green woods
of Fort Worth a cherub met him in a treehouse
and promised the boy he would fly one day.
At least a dozen nights have passed since then
that he was sure was the one he would see
a neighborhood in grids and rows, see like a bird
the way people move among one another,
learn the way Eros maneuvers through the air's ducts,
discover how a hundred red winged horses trample
through a field of clouds. He has traveled

only across the Metroplex where
the glaring lights in Dallas, rays spread
by heavy smog, seem to distract him,
and it's only in the quiet pockets of sky
tucked between a few oaks' peaks
that even hint anymore of letting him fly,
but he'll be damned if a little smog, a few
gunshots, and a city with neurosis
obstruct his flight. Tonight when the widow

next door catches him running after lightning bugs
in his backyard she leans between the peach trees
along the fence and asks him when he will glow
in the dark. He doesn't waste another moment
as the two of them take off

2

to a jazz bistro called Strictly Taboo
where a curly haired woman bellows and
swoons as if wild angels were trapped
in a rhapsody within her throat. With the help
of wild angels, by God, he'll earn his wings or die.

"The Street" Rests
for Robert

Along Elm where Central
cuts through now, where
sidewinders and the city's edges
shopped and hobnobbed
and slept in rooms above
shaky stores, where no tourist
buying at Neiman's dared
to walk or dine not even
to be chic in some quaint café.

Someone owns an Indian Herbal
Shop so neighbors
can get their magic medicine.
Dr. Hamilton works
from the Pythian Temple
as a doctor and a poet
for black freed men's woes
next to where Harry Sigel retails
booze in his first store.

Pawn shop row keeps
business alive, the trade stores
John Neeley Bryan never had.
A "Deep Ellum Special,"
a switchblade knife, a woman
gets her security from Honest Joe
to protect her from men
who get too rough
or who try not to pay.
On a Saturday night,
as Leadbelly plays,
a Jewish furniture maker
locks up his doors tight.

2

If no one is killed
on a Saturday night,
things just ain't going right.

In the main bistro
on "The Street,"
a woman finds
a man to talk to,
glad to be here
sitting with the fan
blowing in
the summer wind,
her feet at rest
as a bass booms the street
awake one more Saturday night.

If no one is killed
on a Saturday night,
things just ain't going right.

In Flight

The Trinity River slices South and North
Dallas, poor and rich, black and white
simplified. I am standing under a bridge
near a levy where an egret stands like stone

paralyzed by the roar of a hundred eighteen-
wheelers and cars at rush hour, its feet
perhaps plastered with concrete festered
from freeways. Somehow with this nude

field of wild grass—this lone stretch of something
left alone only because it has not proven profitable
yet—this bird survives in the Northern shadow
of I. M. Pei's and Philip Johnson's glass pricks.

If only the grass would grow inside my pants,
the bullfrogs leap inside my throat, the unnamed
wildflowers grow inside my nose, I might breathe
and sing a fresh, wild song for this city choking

on its own refrains. I have tried like the red pegasus
coated with soot above the old Mobil headquarters,
to fly in this city, but it only comes in sporadic
patches, half-hearted liftoffs. The egret

suddenly flaps its wings, the current competing
with the undertow of traffic, and soars,
a solemn angel, above the clogged artery of cars.

2

Water Falls
-at McKinney Falls

Something more than sight or grandeur
brings people to these small falls.

Here water still falls and falls still. This phonic
attractor is not nostalgia strumming some doleful
chord. No jukebox melody or refrain gets caught
and lodged in your head for days and dreams.

The sound, though, remains, still, or the memory
of the rush, full and whole and echoing
like the phonic physics of a subway in a tunnel
that has driven itself into the eardrums of a New Yorker.

Hear a prisoner caught in a cinder block chamber
who calls for some human voice and hears
only a steady banging, say, from the basement
heater pipes or his hands slapping the wall.

Somewhere in the nearby woods
a Tonkawa woman screamed her child
into the world and named him "He who moves
with water," This, before McKinney came

and "settled" her and others off the land.
The wails of history are marked in the falls.

Hear the concert in the chambers
of a fetus's world: voices grumble in darkness
on the other side of a warm wall,
the walls themselves churn and grumble
in foreign tongues when the mother's stomach shifts
like Earth's innards, and always the constant drumming
of an echoing heartbeat. Somewhere in a nearby cranny
those sounds still dwell.

In a moment, a man across the creek drinks a beer,
holds his line in the water, as another man
slinks back on his back, reads a book, and a woman
scratches her belly and holds her blond baby's

hand, and the sun, breaking from the clouds
for the fifth or so time today, will slip past the horizon.

All of it falls away with assurance and ease
here where the dead speak clearly.

Sound fills the air. The steadiness is
salvation. The steadiness is.
Steadiness is
what brings us here.

2

Being in Texas

Great thing about being in Texas is you can drive
a few miles outside of Dallas where plastic glass
buildings give room to hills, green and antique,
drunk with teal gray mist, the bashful sun
streaking the streets and fields, and you feel
embarrassingly giddy for a moment as prairies and hills
merge with power lines and metallic Texas instruments,
as bluebonnets and Indian blankets knock you flat,
intoxicated by the smell of wildflowers tapping
on the highway's shoulders,
and you're really not sure where you're at
until the brown specks you know are cows
and the angular wire power towers
whose cords stretch across the freeways
that sneak back to the city
help you get your bearings.

Trying to Get To Sleep

Hold on because nothing nearly came.
At a train depot no one's waiting anymore.
Days of red balloon farewells have slipped
away and remain in general stores near jukeboxes.

Novelty and nostalgia are the United States's cyber-
cinder block. I cannot give you a last line,
a voice says. It's just not right. It would be
forced. I agree and say OK, give me nothing

and I try to doze to sleep. A hand reaches out,
it seems, and taps and taps and taps me,
knuckles caressing my shoulders, and someone is saying Good night. Good night. Good night.

This book designed and produced by Jennifer Polavieja in Dallas, Texas.
The text is Cheltenham Light nine on twelve. Poem titles are Geometric Medium.
Belwe was used on title pages and Granjon was used in some of the introductory pages.